I0440169

AI:

ACTIVATE your IMAGINATION
&
AMPLIFY your INTELLIGENCE

#ACTIVATEyourIMAGINATIONAI
#AMPLIFYyourINTELLIGENCEAI

The digital late learner and tech-novice's guide to practical ways **Artificial Intelligence (AI) can** immediately improve your life.

Dr. Arthur L.C. Antoine, PE, PMP, DBIA

Copyright © 2024 Arthur Antoine

All rights reserved.

DEDICATION

Regardless of generational title and the inherent speculations about attitudes to technology, this eBook is designed for the...

Tech-Curious Individual

Technology Exploring Adult

New Digital Learner

Tech-Novice

"It has become appallingly obvious that our technology has exceeded our humanity."

- Albert Einstein

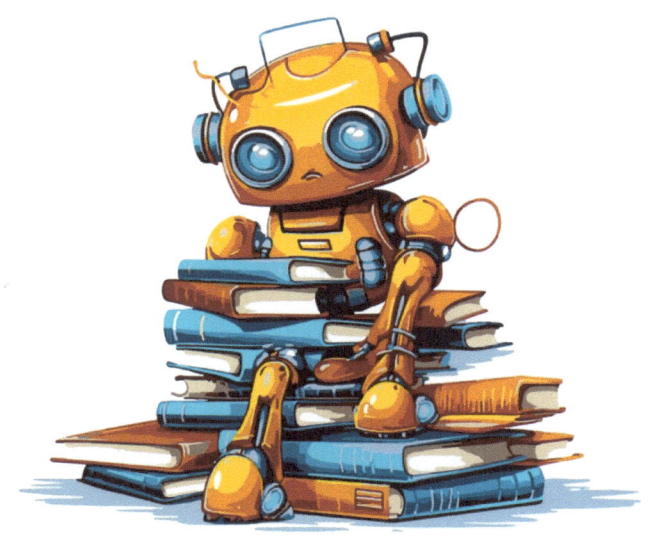

Table
of Contents

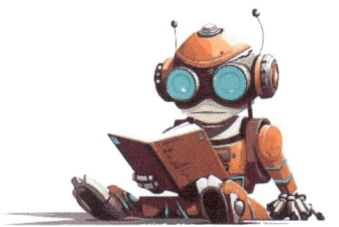

Introduction

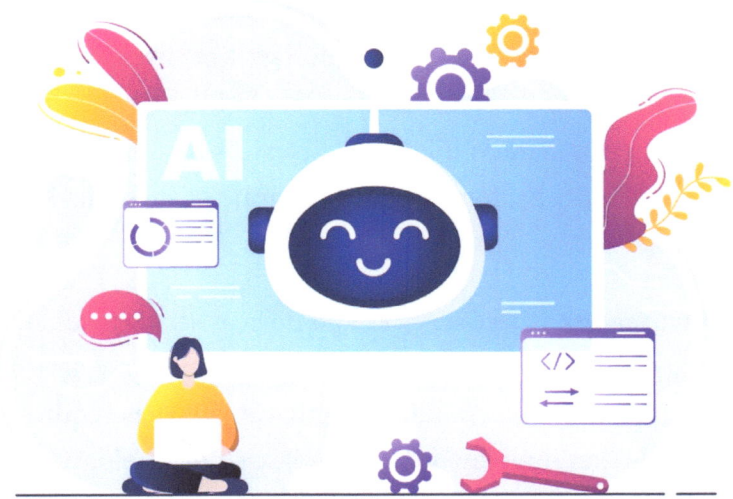

The race is on amongst the major players in the tech/online nexus to create the next new Artificial Intelligence (AI) hit. Lead by companies such as Google, OpenAI, Microsoft, along with a host of other startup companies, these companies all aim to grab a share of the open market of prospective users globally who are eager to get their hands on new technology and new AI featured devices.

Unless you've literally been under-a-rock somewhere or a detractor for whatever reason, AI is here and here to stay. I'm no futurist, rather, I consider myself an optimist of the prospects that lay ahead in the rapidly changing world of the new economic frontier i.e., technology and online services.

The use and prospects of AI are already mimicking trends of previous global technology stalwarts that have outlasted the waves of fear, criticism, denial, to global acceptance as irreplaceable parts of our lives; perfect example your mobile/smart phone, which has become an extra artificial limb for some of us.

Furthermore, the global tech leaders have been incrementally dosing us with lesser sophisticated AI technology like Siri on your iPhone, Google Assistant as integrated into Google Maps, and other smart-speaker/home-assistant WiFi devices. Devices that everyone seems to love, except me [smh], for some reason none of these devices get my accent.

Notice that many of these services and devices serve the dual purpose of meeting our convenient needs while, at the same time, feeding these same tech leaders and corporations with the data they require from us in order to further innovate more complex AI technology.

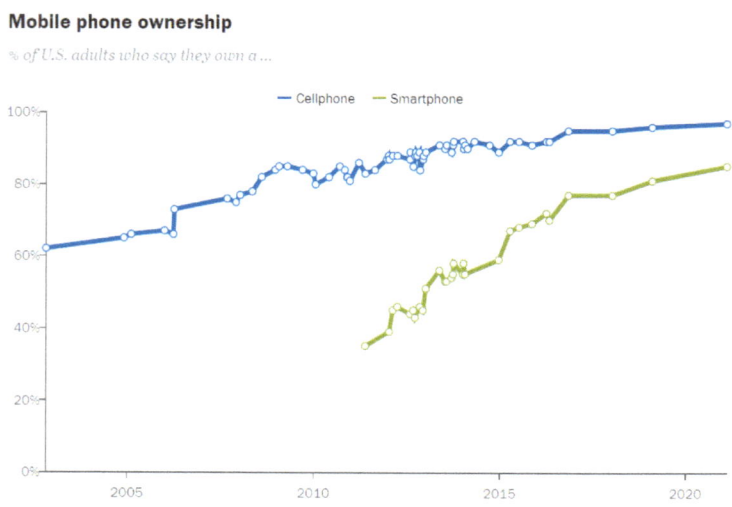

Mobile phone ownership

% of U.S. adults who say they own a ...

Source: Surveys of U.S. adults conducted 2002-2021.

PEW RESEARCH CENTER

U.S. Artificial Intelligence Market Size 2022 to 2032

Source: Precedence Research

In any case, for the new digital learners and tech novices, here's a definition in my layman's terms –

Artificial Intelligence, aka AI, is a developed computer systems or machine that can perform tasks that typically require human intelligence – objectively, it aims to recreate or substitute the human brain *[more on the repercussions of this feat later]* in functioning tasks at incredible speed.

These tasks may include learning, reasoning, problem-solving, perception, understanding natural language, and more...

Newer AI technology, e.g., generative AI, is even claimed to be able to recreate sound, imagery, and literature at the expert level of esteemed artistes on command by users.

By simulating these basic and complex human cognitive abilities in machines, enabling them to analyze data, adapt to new information, and make decisions or predictions, create works of art, etc. possibilities are limitless.

AI undoubtedly will disrupt many sectors, if not all, from healthcare to finance to how we socialize and travel, etc. Already, educators are struggling to pivot in the already shaken up world of institutionalized learning. Teachers who may be nay-sayers and reluctant to recognize the need to shift from teaching kids to learn based on a deliverable that can instantly and authentically be produced by AI will fall by the wayside. As an alternative these teachers should start to consider how learning could be enhanced by teaching kids better processes of thinking and solving real-world problems. Additionally, teachers should consider innovative ways that AI can be used in classrooms.

Personally, I am eager to see how AI affects the so-called "Third World", i.e., how AI will improve or further widen the economic gap between developed countries and small island developing states like those of my home region, the Caribbean. In the context of developing nations globally, nations that may already be facing significant economic and social challenges exacerbated by the effects of the pandemic-era, I can only hope that relevant authorities focus on establishing frameworks and procedures to effectively manage, operate, and supervise the deployment of AI systems through the lens of good governance, value to citizenry, and transparency. As governments reel and brace for impact who knows what may unfold. Rest assured, we can ALWAYS rely on government to impose the legislation we need, right...

Now, here comes the catch...

What happens when we substitute the human brain you ask?

My best analogy to answer this question is that of any typical team sport where the substituted player has to revert to idly sit on the bench and watch the rest of the game. What's that popular phrase about idle minds again?? Go ask an AI system!!

Now, I don't know about you, however, as an ex-avid-Football player *[to specify, I intentionally avoid the "S"-word].* A player and fanatic at various levels, although under 5'-7" and max. 130lbs, I never spent time on the bench of any team that I chose to play for, in some of the notoriously toughest local district leagues.

I had to think to find a way to be the first choice of coaches in the Defensive-Midfield role so I became valued for being able to read the game and quickly analyze the situation, positional shape of my teammates around me, and react accordingly to coach's instructions or just wing-it for best success.

In that role my contribution to the game was more important than explosive dribbling or brainless heavy tackling skills. Instead, my duty was to provide a consistent presence laterally across the field to stop the opposition's play by making the first tackle, ensure my team kept as much possession of the ball as possible and coordinate my team's shape by constant communication with other defensive midfielders *[i.e., if an option in the formation - RIP Dave!] and* with defensive center-backs.

I totally digressed there, however, the point is don't get kicked out the game, it's time to think of how you can stay in the action with the starting/front-line team.

With the pace of technology only expected to exponentially increase, you can't afford to miss out on AI. For instance, according to tech-guru Dr. Kai-Fu Lee, one of the most prominent figures in the global AI community, AI is predicted to decrease repetitive jobs for both blue-collar and white-collar workers; "over 40% of jobs globally will be displaceable."

It's time to step up your game, **Activate** your **Imagination,** try to **Amplify** your **Intelligence** and keep up with the action!

Practical Applications and Recommendations

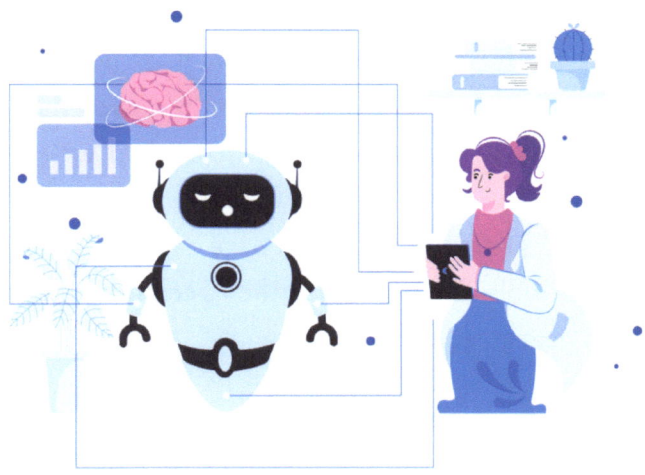

T his book was inspired by casual conversations with colleagues whose professions, like mine, are external to the tech/online world, yet we nerd-out at the prospects of new technology and the global impacts.

Further, serving as a guest lecturer at a local university and being enmeshed in my local community as an advocate to help "New Americans" (i.e., foreign students, and experienced migrant professionals) integrate socially and culturally in the US STEM landscape, my interactions as a volunteer academic coach and career mentor revealed that many individuals at all ages were taking the AI phenomenon for granted.

As such, I felt the need to present in a simple format, practical examples of how AI can be used to improve aspects of our daily lives.

I thought firstly of my deceased Mother's inherent curious nature. She would have been in her early-70's at this time. Despite the hours I may have had to spend explaining use of the technology to her initially, I'm sure she would have been intrigued at the ability to call up any global desert recipe at will for her burgeoning catering business using AI.

As such, inspired by the memory of her inquisitiveness I was motivated to draft this eBook, designed for displaying the ease of AI's use for any daily task or query. It's structured as an easy-read for anyone who may have grown up in a time when technology wasn't as prevalent and for those who might not have had the same exposure or access to digital tools and devices as the "Technoholics" of younger generations in developed nations.

Getting straight to it, I present some practical applications and recommendations by interesting categories with brief narrative and simple screenshot examples to hopefully trigger your imagination for applying AI to your needs.

Firstly, a key concept worth grasping for use of any AI or software system is **prompt engineering**. The saying goes, "Garbage-In, Garbage-Out." By prompt engineering, you should recognize that the quality of your interaction with an AI system will depend on the quality of your input query to said system. In other words, how you make your request of the AI system will determine the system's interpretation of your needs and the resulting output.

Lately, there's a plethora of full courses available online just on prompt engineering. To simplify the concept for the Non-Tech Native savvy individual who's eager to jump into using AI. Let's take a simple example of Mom searching for a catering recipe. Notice here in the screenshots provided, the level of granularity in the detail between the prompts as "How to Bake a cake?" versus "How to bake a cake quickly like an experienced chef?"

Try experimenting for yourself with a new prompt such as "How to bake a cake with chocolate icing quickly in 5 steps?" or any prompt of your own design. There's no harm to the system and you won't break it. In fact, I'm sure you'll be intrigued by the system's response should your new prompt be inappropriate in some way or even practically impossible. Be forewarned, in such cases, don't take it personal.

AR

You

How to bake a cake?

ChatGPT

ChatGPT

Baking a cake can be a delightful process! Here's a simple recipe to get you started:

Ingredients:

- **2 cups (250g) all-purpose flour**
- **1 ½ cups (300g) granulated sugar**
- **1 cup (240ml) milk**
- **½ cup (120ml) vegetable oil**
- **2 large eggs**
- **2 teaspoons baking powder**
- **1 teaspoon vanilla extract**
- **A pinch of salt**

Instructions:

1. **Preparation:**

   - Preheat your oven to 350°F (180°C).
   - Grease and flour two 9-inch round cake pans.

2. **Mix Dry Ingredients:**

   - In a bowl, whisk together the flour, baking powder, and salt.

3. Combine Wet Ingredients:

- In a separate bowl, whisk together the sugar, eggs, oil, milk, and vanilla extract until well combined.

4. Combine Mixtures:

- Gradually add the dry ingredients into the wet ingredients, mixing until the batter is smooth and there are no lumps.

5. Bake:

- Pour the batter evenly into the prepared cake pans.
- Place them in the preheated oven and bake for about 25-30 minutes or until a toothpick inserted into the center of the cakes comes out clean.

6. Cooling:

- Once done, remove the cakes from the oven and let them cool in the pans for about 10 minutes.
- Then, transfer the cakes onto a wire rack to cool completely before frosting.

You can frost the cake with your choice of frosting, whether it's classic buttercream, cream cheese frosting, chocolate ganache, or any other favorite.

Remember, baking times can vary based on your oven, so keep an eye on the cakes as they bake! Enjoy the process and the delicious results!

You

How to bake a cake quickly like an experienced chef?

ChatGPT

ChatGPT

Absolutely, experienced chefs often have a few tricks up their sleeves to speed up the cake baking process without sacrificing quality. Here are some tips to bake a cake quickly:

1. Gather Ingredients and Tools First:

- Before starting, ensure you have all the ingredients and equipment ready. Measure the ingredients precisely to streamline the process.

2. Room Temperature Ingredients:

- Use room temperature ingredients, especially eggs and butter. Cold ingredients can slow down mixing and affect the cake's texture.

3. One-Bowl Method:

- Instead of using separate bowls for dry and wet ingredients, some chefs combine everything in one bowl. Start with the dry ingredients, then add the wet ingredients gradually while mixing.

4. Use Self-Rising Flour:

- Self-rising flour contains baking powder and salt, reducing the need for measuring and adding them separately.

5. Increase Oven Temperature Slightly:

- Some chefs slightly increase the oven temperature to bake the cake faster without compromising the texture. However, monitor the cake closely to prevent over-browning or drying out.

6. Smaller, Thinner Layers:

- Bake the cake in smaller, thinner layers to reduce baking time. Instead of two tall layers, consider making three or four thinner ones.

7. Convection Bake:

- If your oven has a convection setting, use it. Convection baking circulates hot air, cooking the cake faster and more evenly.

8. Use Hot Water or Coffee:

- Adding hot water or coffee to the batter can expedite the baking process, as it helps activate the leavening agents more quickly.

9. Preheating Time:

- Ensure the oven is properly preheated before putting the cake batter in. This ensures the cake starts baking immediately.

10. Choose Quick Frosting Methods:

- Opt for quick frosting methods, like simple glazes or dusting the cake with powdered sugar, to avoid waiting for elaborate frostings to set.

11. Microwave Techniques:

- In some cases, chefs use microwaves for initial heating of certain ingredients like butter or milk to speed up the process. However, this technique requires careful monitoring to avoid overheating.

12. Chilled Cake Layering:

- If time permits, chilling the cake layers in the freezer for a short time (15-20 minutes) can make them easier to handle and assemble.

By combining these techniques, you can significantly reduce the time required to bake a cake while maintaining a delicious outcome. Keep an eye on the cake as it bakes, adjusting times and temperatures as needed.

Communication - Linguistics/Language

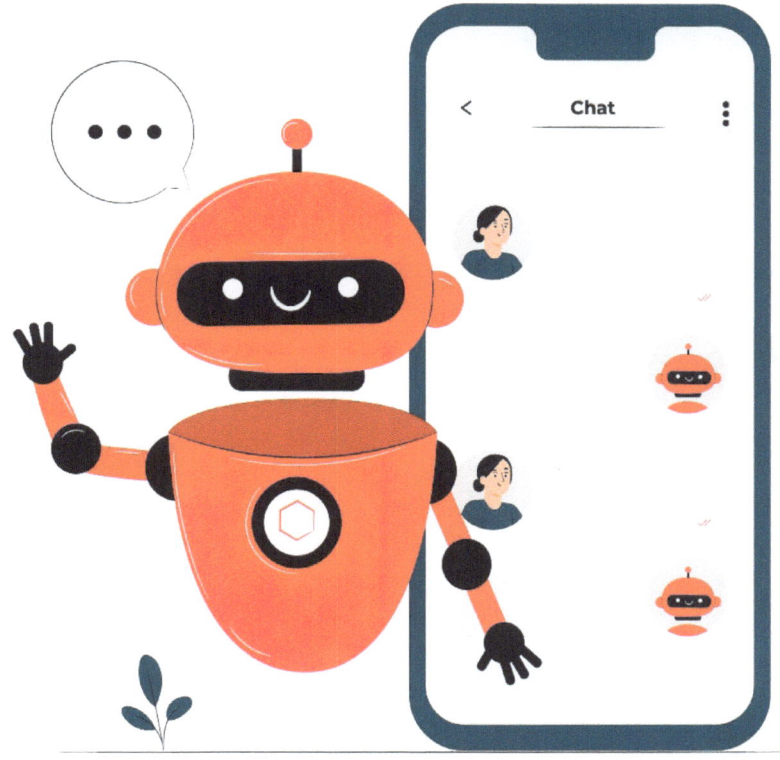

One morning, I shared breakfast with an accomplished engineer who was forced to migrate to the US from Afghanistan. A seasoned professional from overseas, his move to the US wasn't by choice and he found himself displaced into a whole new world, adapting and learning to navigate unfamiliar US

DEI issues, social and cultural norms, with the added burden of learning a new language; all with the aim of regaining full-time employment in a role at his level of expertise rather than being unemployed or underemployed.

Despite being in a legal-to-work immigration status the best jobs he could obtain besides driving Uber all day were technician level field work. Notably, he liked Uber as he got to practice English and social interactions.

As a new learner of English his pace and intonation needed refinement, more so, his writing skills as I recognized from emails and text correspondence. I thought, why not show him how to use Chat GPT on his mobile phone to better structure his sentences to improve his written communication. After all, if he could write better it should lead to his speaking improving, in addition to helping reduce errors when he's working on his job applications in a silo.

Lo and behold, I shared with him a single prompt after he install the app on his mobile phone and I was surprised at how he was truly amazed at the prospects, saving the prompt verbatim in his phone's notes.

Within weeks, thankfully, he was in a better job. I'm unsure if it was a result of my advice, however, it wouldn't have hurt to help. Here's a simple example of how AI can not only provide direct translations, it can further refine the phrase and terminology to match the context of what is attempting to be said.

AR

You

Refine my English: what one are they using?

ChatGPT

ChatGPT

Certainly! Here's a refined version: "Which option are they utilizing?"

AR

You

digame en Espanol

ChatGPT

ChatGPT

Claro, la frase "¿Cuál están utilizando?"

AR

You

Now in french

ChatGPT

ChatGPT

Bien sûr, en français, votre question était : "Lequel utilisent-ils ?"

AR

You

provide it in Mandarin (Chinese)

ChatGPT

ChatGPT

The translation of "Which option are they utilizing?" to Mandarin Chinese is:

他们在使用哪个选项？(Tāmen zài shǐyòng nǎge xuǎnxiàng?)

Marketing

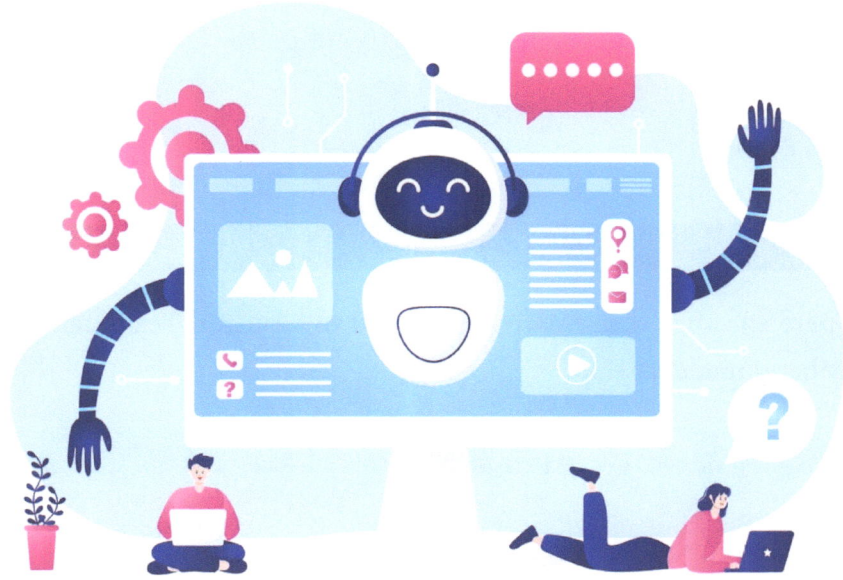

A I's role in home business marketing presents another landscape of possibilities. By leveraging AI-driven analytics, small and large businesses can gain deeper insights into consumer behavior, preferences, and trends. These insights enable personalized marketing strategies tailored to individual customers and communities, leading to more effective and targeted campaigns to help businesses anticipate customer needs, optimize pricing strategies, and suggest personalized product recommendations.

Furthermore, online businesses are already using AI chatbots and virtual assistants to enhance customer interactions and minimize employee workloads by providing instant support using AI to answer queries, and guide customers through their purchase journey or to resolve problems.

As AI continues to evolve, home businesses stand to benefit from its ability to streamline marketing efforts, improve customer engagement, and drive revenue growth by delivering tailored and impactful marketing initiatives. Consider a new market for your hobby:

AR

You

Where specifically in my neighborhood of Houston Texas can I sell my hand made hats?

ChatGPT

ChatGPT

Finding specific locations in your neighborhood of Houston, Texas, might require local knowledge or direct research, as it can vary based on the area. However, here are some general strategies to pinpoint places where you can sell your handmade hats:

Local Craft Stores and Boutiques:

- Explore nearby craft stores, fashion boutiques, or consignment shops. These places often support local artisans and might be interested in showcasing and selling your handmade hats.

Farmers Markets and Artisan Fairs:

- Visit local farmers markets or artisan fairs. These events often feature booths for handmade crafts and might offer you a platform to display and sell your hats.

Community Centers and Events:

- Check with local community centers, churches, or event venues in your neighborhood. They might organize events, fairs, or gatherings where you can set up a booth to sell your hats.

Online Platforms with Local Focus:

- Utilize online platforms like social media groups specific to your Houston neighborhood or neighborhood-specific marketplaces where you can advertise and sell your hats to local residents.

Networking and Local Groups:

- Connect with local artisans, crafters, or neighborhood associations. They might offer insights into specific locations or events where handmade items like yours are sold.

To find specific locations in your neighborhood, consider reaching out to local business associations or artisan groups, asking for recommendations from fellow artisans, or exploring local community bulletin boards, which often display information about local markets or events. Additionally, conducting online searches using keywords like "handmade crafts markets in [your neighborhood]" might provide specific locations where you can sell your hats in Houston.

Security
& Surveillance

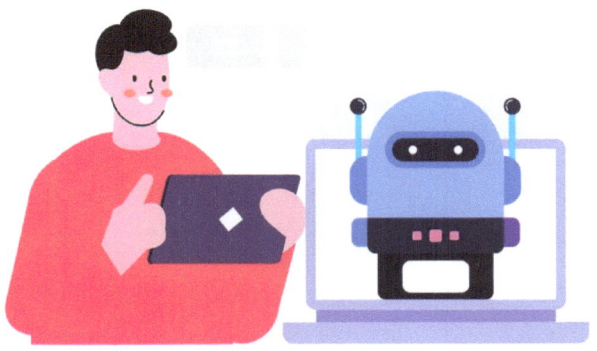

A I is already revolutionizing security and surveillance by enabling real-time video analytics for object detection and behavioral analysis, deploying facial recognition for identification, and employing predictive analytics to foresee potential threats. These systems generate automated alerts, integrate with smart cameras and drones, and enhance cybersecurity measures, ushering in a proactive approach to threat detection and response.

As AI evolves, it promises improved accuracy, and seamless integration with existing security infrastructure, shaping a future where safety and privacy coexist harmoniously. Of course, ethical considerations will need to be implemented in the extent of use to maintain our privacy.

Meantime, for some added security at home feel free to prompt for some insight e.g.:

AR

You

How can I secure my door from burglars?

ChatGPT

ChatGPT

Securing your door is crucial in preventing burglaries. Here are some effective ways to bolster your door's security:

1. Upgrade Locks:

- Install high-quality deadbolts with long bolts that extend deep into the door frame. Grade 1 deadbolts offer the highest level of security.

2. Reinforce Door Frames:

- Strengthen weak points around the door frame by using longer screws to secure the strike plate, hinges, and frame to the wall studs.

3. Use Security Bars or Grilles:

- Consider installing security bars or grilles over glass panels or sidelights to prevent intruders from breaking the glass and reaching in to unlock the door.

4. Smart Locks:

- Invest in smart locks that offer additional features like keyless entry, remote locking/unlocking, and activity logs. Some models can be integrated with home security systems.

Agriculture

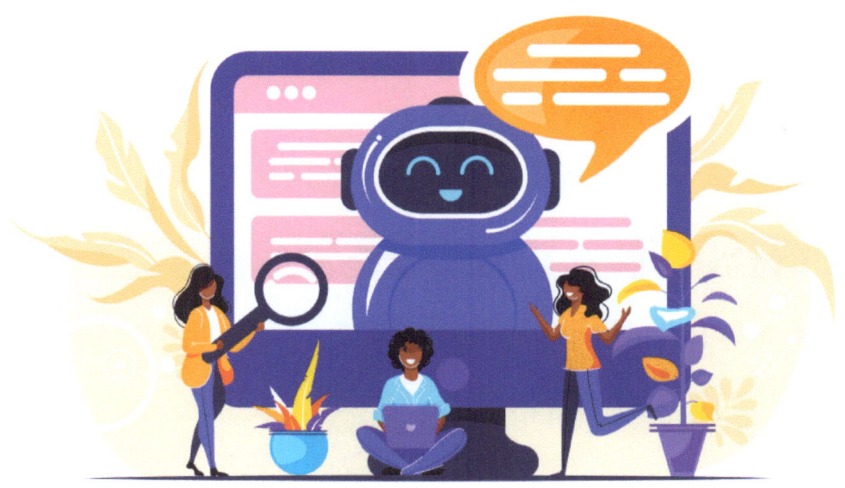

Imagine the use of AI in agriculture coupled with drone technology! This presents a transformative future by optimizing farming practices through data-driven insights. Drones equipped with AI sensors and imaging technology can facilitate precision agriculture, capturing high-resolution data on crop health, soil conditions, and irrigation needs.

AI algorithms can analyze this data, offering farmers actionable insights, enabling precise pesticide application, efficient water usage, and targeted crop monitoring. Furthermore, AI-powered predictive analytics forecast weather patterns, crop diseases, and yield predictions, empowering farmers to make informed decisions for increased productivity and sustainability. As technology advances, the integration of AI and drones holds the promise of revolutionizing farming practices, minimizing resource wastage, and ensuring global food security in an ever-changing agricultural landscape. A particularly exciting feature for the self-sustainability of developing nations!

For now, let's save a house plant:

You

Home made tips to keep my dracanea alive while I'm gone traveling?

ChatGPT

ChatGPT

Absolutely! Here are some homemade tips to help keep your Dracaena healthy while you're away traveling:

1. Self-Watering System:

- Create a simple self-watering system by placing one end of a cotton string or fabric strip in a container of water and burying the other end in the soil of your Dracaena. The soil will draw up moisture as needed, keeping the plant hydrated.

2. Watering Globes or Bottles:

- Use water-filled globes or small bottles with pin-sized holes in the cap. Invert them and insert them into the soil near the plant's roots. They will slowly release water as the soil dries out.

3. Humidity Trays:

- Place your Dracaena pot on a humidity tray filled with water and pebbles. As the water evaporates, it increases humidity around the plant, helping it retain moisture.

4. Plastic Bag Method:

- Before leaving, water the plant thoroughly and enclose it in a large, clear plastic bag. Seal the bag around the pot to create a mini-greenhouse effect. This can help maintain moisture levels.

5. Soak the Soil:

- Water the plant thoroughly just before your departure. Ensure the soil is evenly moist but not waterlogged. This can sustain the plant for a while by providing ample moisture.

6. Group Plants Together:

- If you have multiple plants, clustering them together can create a microclimate with higher humidity, helping to retain moisture.

7. Reduce Sunlight Exposure:

- Move the plant away from direct sunlight or areas prone to drafts to reduce water loss through evaporation.

8. Mulch:

- Add a layer of mulch (like sphagnum moss or coconut coir) on top of the soil to reduce moisture evaporation.

Kids Off-Screen Entertainment

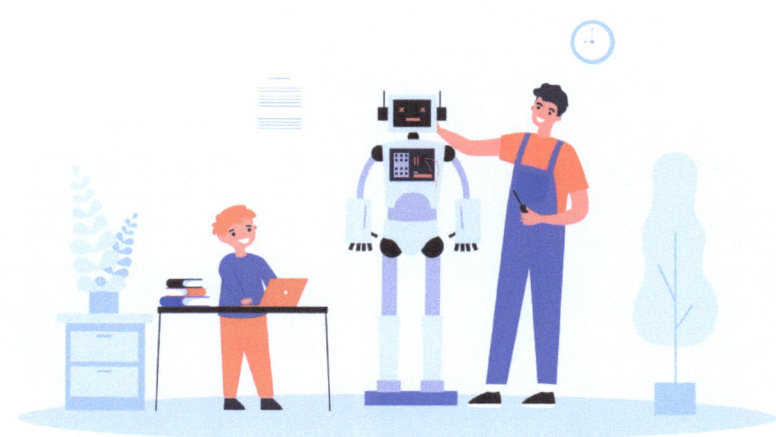

We're truly in our new era of social atrophy worldwide, typically it's blamed on technology; we're all included. Take for example our toddlers and younger youth who are already learning to navigate touchscreen programs for instantaneous short-lived gratification.

Even adults are reluctant to return to in-person work spaces preferring the hybrid and remote work conveniences rely on technological collaboration tools for instant messaging and virtual meetings. It's doubtful that we recognize the social isolation that these tools foster and resulting impacts on our human evolution.

Notably, he U.S. Surgeon General's released an advisory report detailing why social connection matters in our relationships and interactions, not limited to family, friends, colleagues, neighbors, etc. In this 2023 report titled "Our Epidemic of Loneliness and Isolation,"

Dr. Vivek H. Murthy the 19th and 21st Surgeon General of the US points out that *"lacking social connection can increase the risk for premature death as much as smoking up to 15 cigarettes a day."*

On the brighter side, consider using AI for more options for off-screen interaction time with and among our youngsters.

Here's a useful example for the next time you run out of that commercially provided bubble-making liquid for that toy your 2-year-old just NEEDS to stay distracted while you attend that online Zoom meeting and you don't have time to rush to the nearest store:

AR

You

provide best proportion mix of dish washing liquid to water for toy bubble maker

ChatGPT

ChatGPT

For a toy bubble maker, the ideal proportion of dishwashing liquid to water is roughly 1 part dish soap to 6 parts water. This ratio tends to create a solution that produces long-lasting bubbles without being too diluted or too concentrated. However, you might need to adjust the ratio slightly based on the specific toy bubble maker and the desired bubble size and longevity.

Spirituality & Religion

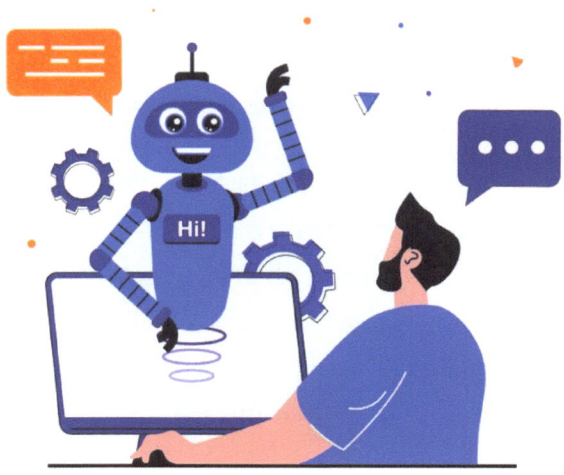

I feel like it would be remiss of me to exclude religion as an ode to Mom; she was a fervent God-believer and devoted church-goer. Throughout our travels, I do recall my youthful queries with reluctance to join her at religious services certain times. In response she'd candidly admit that her selection of the church or religious institution of the day was a matter of convenience. As such she would drag me, her only kid, along to the nearest religious house with open doors; in hindsight, the experiences offered great exposure to my youthful developing mind.

For the spiritual and/or religiously inclined individual new to the technology. I confess, I have no idea if your omni-present deity of preference is in the shell of the AI technology. I leave that discovery and determination to you.

However, I do propose that you dispel any reluctance of using AI and try it for yourself. Try to reference and compare the AI results to any of your great books be it your book of Barnabas, Testaments, Quran, Bhagavad Gita in any of the various original languages.

You may be fascinated by the access to such content at your fingertips!

Or charmed by the ability to draft that awe-inspiring sermon or message on some topic which you've been waiting to hear about!

On a more pragmatic note, as much as social atrophy plagues us lately, consider whether you can improve your day-to-day interpersonal skills and interactions with others by AMPLIFYING YOUR INTELLIGENCE. Try using AI for a quick second thought about your reactions when triggered or to discern what action to take when facing some ethical or moral dilemma instead of resorting to rash or impulsive reactions.

AR

You

Provide a verse from the Quran: Ayat al-Kursi

ChatGPT

ChatGPT

Certainly! Ayat al-Kursi, also known as "The Throne Verse," is one of the most well-known and revered verses in the Quran, found in Surah Al-Baqarah (Chapter 2), verse 255. Here is the English translation:

"Allah! There is no deity except Him, the Ever-Living, the Sustainer of existence. Neither drowsiness overtakes Him nor sleep. To Him belongs whatever is in the heavens and whatever is on the earth. Who is it that can intercede with Him except by His permission? He knows what is [presently] before them and what will be after them, and they encompass not a thing of His knowledge except for what He wills. His Kursi [throne] extends over the heavens and the earth, and their preservation tires Him not. And He is the Most High, the Most Great."

This verse is highly regarded for its emphasis on the greatness of God, His attributes, and His sovereignty over all creation.

AR

You

Can you provide it in it's original language

ChatGPT

ChatGPT

Certainly! Here is Ayat al-Kursi in Arabic:

اللَّهُ لَا إِلَٰهَ إِلَّا هُوَ الْحَيُّ الْقَيُّومُ ۚ لَا تَأْخُذُهُ سِنَةٌ وَلَا نَوْمٌ ۚ لَهُ مَا فِي السَّمَاوَاتِ وَمَا فِي الْأَرْضِ ۗ مَنْ ذَا الَّذِي يَشْفَعُ عِنْدَهُ إِلَّا بِإِذْنِهِ ۚ يَعْلَمُ مَا بَيْنَ أَيْدِيهِمْ وَمَا خَلْفَهُمْ ۖ وَلَا يُحِيطُونَ بِشَيْءٍ مِنْ عِلْمِهِ إِلَّا بِمَا شَاءَ ۚ وَسِعَ كُرْسِيُّهُ السَّمَاوَاتِ وَالْأَرْضَ ۖ وَلَا يَئُودُهُ حِفْظُهُمَا ۚ وَهُوَ الْعَلِيُّ الْعَظِيمُ

This verse is highly significant in Islamic tradition and is frequently recited for its spiritual and protective value.

AR

You

Give a popular verse from Bhagavad Gita

ChatGPT

ChatGPT

One of the most famous and often quoted verses from the Bhagavad Gita, a revered Hindu scripture, is from Chapter 2, Verse 47:

"कर्मण्येवाधिकारस्ते मा फलेषु कदाचन । मा कर्मफलहेतुर्भूर्मा ते सङ्गोऽस्त्वकर्मणि ॥"

This verse can be transliterated as:

"Karmanye vadhikaraste Ma Phaleshu Kadachana Ma Karma Phala Hetur Bhurmatey Sangostva Akarmani"

And in English, a common translation is:

"You have a right to perform your prescribed duties, but you are not entitled to the fruits of your actions. Never consider yourself to be the cause of the results of your activities, nor be attached to inaction."

This verse is often cited to emphasize the importance of focusing on performing one's duties or responsibilities without being attached to the outcomes or results. It teaches the principle of detached action, emphasizing the performance of duty for its own sake without being concerned about the rewards or consequences.

Moral dilemma with your friend you say?

My friend borrowed $1000 and promised to pay me in 2 days, it's been 2 weeks, what would Jesus do

ChatGPT

ChatGPT

In situations like this, Jesus often advocated for forgiveness, understanding, and compassion. He taught about love, mercy, and the importance of treating others as you would want to be treated. Here are some principles that might guide your decision:

1. **Patience and Understanding:** Jesus often encouraged patience and understanding. Consider reaching out to your friend to inquire about the situation calmly and understandingly. There might be reasons for the delay that you're not aware of.

2. **Forgiveness and Compassion:** Jesus spoke about forgiveness and compassion. If your friend is facing difficulties, consider showing compassion and being willing to forgive the debt or work out a different arrangement that's fair to both of you.

3. **Communication and Resolution:** It's important to communicate your concerns respectfully. Express the impact of the delay on you and try to find a resolution that both honors your needs and understands their situation.

While it's crucial to uphold your own rights and responsibilities, Jesus' teachings often emphasize compassion, forgiveness, and understanding in dealing with others, especially in matters involving debts or obligations. It's about finding a balance between fairness and mercy.

AR

You

Provide a short relevant Bible verse

ChatGPT

ChatGPT

Certainly! Here's a short and relevant Bible verse from the book of Colossians, Chapter 3, Verse 13:

"Bear with each other and forgive one another if any of you has a grievance against someone. Forgive as the Lord forgave you."

This verse emphasizes the importance of patience, forgiveness, and understanding in our interactions with others, reflecting the teachings of Jesus about forgiveness and compassion.

Conclusion

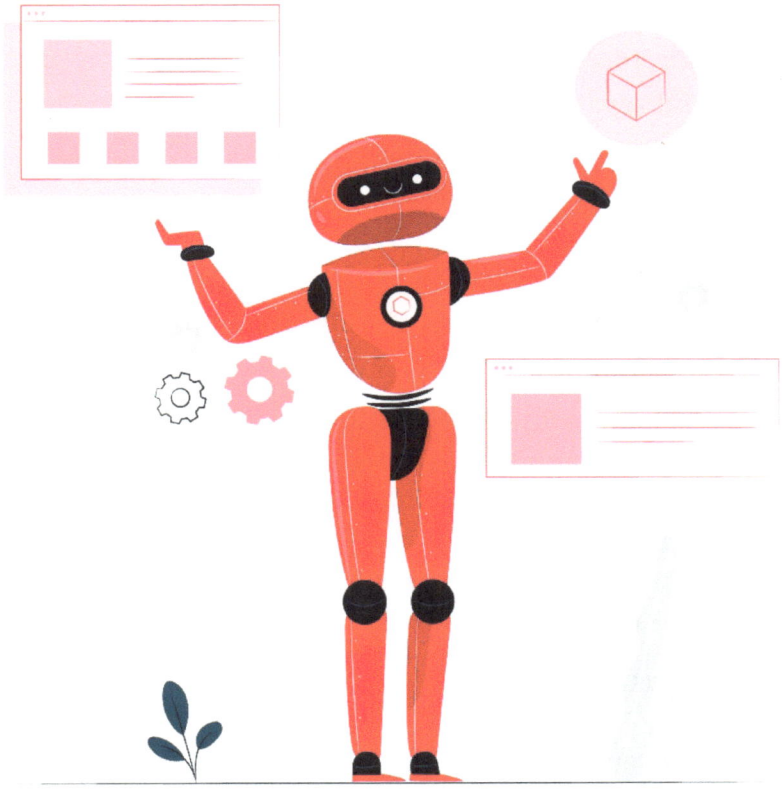

T hrough this brief journey exploring the possibilities of AI for new digital learners and tech-novices, I hope that it triggered a sense of optimism and inspiration to dive in, to access the technology and test for yourself the limitless possibilities.

There are many other sectors that will undoubtedly be improved for humanity's brighter future, where AI and technology empowers us to overcome challenges, create new solutions, and foster positive change.

Just think of the possibilities of AI coupled with specialized healthcare for better and more efficient cancer eradication techniques, or customized learning curricula for developing individual student's talents, or intelligent traffic management systems for smart cities.

At the same time there will certainly be disruption in many sectors, as has been the precedent set with every evolutionary step in global technological advancement, from the use of fire to electricity, scribes to machine printing, horses to auto-mobiles, and telegraph to the internet.

Personally, at this early onset of the release of various AI technology tools, I've noticed as if there is an Inherent hesitation, an awkward pause to weigh the ethics of use. Even in casual conversations with peers it seems like an admission of using AI for whatever purpose implies that you're using less brain power.

Despite the naysayers and reluctant purists, to the adventurous and creative spirit, I say go forth, be bold, seize the moment to create and discover at will, in speed and bounds, knowing confidently that your mind is still in the game!

I suggest that you be proud to admit that yes, you do indeed find ways to **ACTIVATE YOUR IMAGINATION** and use available technological innovation as tools to **AMPLIFY YOUR INTELLIGENCE.**

Of course, ethical concerns are valid in certain sectors. The business sectors I feel for the most are the creative industry and institutionalized religion.

What's going to happen to our creative industry? In particular, will we get cheaper, mass produced versions of written literature, visual art, and music accessible to our various individual preferences and transient emotions? With technology designed to learn and instantly reproduce artistic work at the level of our historic and current human greats, who knows what's to become of such inherently revered talent and human productions.

With religion, could my 2-year-old daughter or 3-year-old son be instantly directed to connect with their soul-mate in some other remote part of the world by the click of a button? Within the next couple decades or less, will they be getting married with the wedding officiated by an AI priest who provides an eloquent ceremonial sermon unique to their union?

In conclusion, there's no need to be dismayed! As dire as it may seem to some of us, our collective human intellect always transcends!

Already in my professional role in the construction and engineering industry, I'm recognizing a refreshing shift of focus to the softer side of things rather than the heavy scientific aspects and technical knowledge. I'm noticing more emotional intelligence and collaborative skills training options arise. For instance, the perpetual development of project delivery methods (contracting methods) is shifting to more collaborative models that bring the contractual parties together in a seamless, less adversarial manner for project success. This phenomenon is happening globally, from Australia to the UK and US, pioneering models such as Early Contractor Involvement (ECI), Integrated Project Delivery (IPD), Alliancing, and the UK's intriguing Project 13 enterprise model.

Intrigued by the possibilities the future holds, I can't wait till AI can pick up the kids, mow the lawn, fix dinner, take out the trash, and get the dishes done 😊

AI:

ACTIVATE your IMAGINATION
&
AMPLIFY your INTELLIGENCE
#ACTIVATEyourIMAGINATIONAI
#AMPLIFYyourINTELLIGENCEAI

The digital late learner and tech-novice's guide to practical ways **Artificial Intelligence (AI)** can immediately improve your life.

About the Author

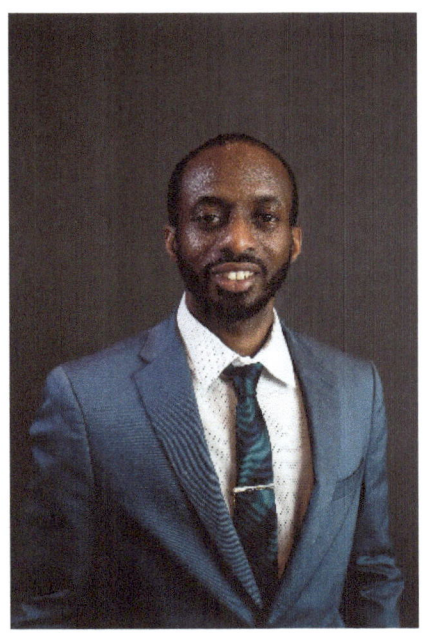

Dr. Antoine has over 20 years of experience as a civil engineer and project manager. As an academic, he has conducted extensive research in his field, making significant contributions to the body of knowledge on project delivery methods and procurement, in particular, collaborative project delivery methods. His passions for service and research are as follows, **Program/Project Management** – specialist for large multidisciplinary project teams**, Collaboration specialist** – adept at consensus building and nurturing cohesive functional teams**, STEM Education Advocacy & Academic/Career Coaching -** particularly for under-represented minorities and the citizenry of developing nations. Along with his expertise he offers a diverse perspective to solutions with his global experience. Dr. Antoine has worked for multinational engineering consultants where he has been tasked with civil engineering and project management duties, in all stages of project lifecycles from inception through to monitoring and closeout, to deliver projects that exceeded aligned expectations.

Contact the Author

Feel free to reach out if any issues/queries/guidance needed or just for an exploratory chat:

Arthur Antoine, PhD, PE, PMP, DBIA
Civil Engineer & Senior Project Manager
Personal email: A1.EngineeringSLU@Gmail.com
C: 917-645-2095

LinkedIn: https://www.linkedin.com/in/arthur-antoine-phd-pe-pmp-dbia-64203712b

Disclaimer

This Book was created by dictated voice recordings to OpenAI's ChatGPT 3.5 phone app & copy-paste editing to Microsoft Word format for publication. The preceding content was made from 100% original human thought and initiative supported by extracted AI example screenshots of usage.

While there are many other AI options available, the included example screenshots of AI use were extracted from OpenAI's ChatGPT 3.5 system as a matter of convenience and for consistent display for ease or readers new to the subject.

Except for English, other languages and symbol outputs from AI have not been checked to confirm accuracy besides transfer to other AI free translate software e.g. Google Translate. Furthermore, be forewarned of the possibility of inaccuracies and "hallucinations" in the responses provided from any AI technology. It's worthwhile to fact check from a relevant source; these may soon become indistinguishable as AI is further unleashed.

Interesting resources

64 Artificial Intelligence (AI) Companies to Know by Built In.

AI Superpowers: China, Silicon Valley and the New World Order, book by Dr. Kai-Fu Lee 2018.

Artificial Intelligence, full episodes by 60 Minutes.

Artificial Intelligence's Use and Rapid Growth Highlight Its Possibilities and Perils by the U.S. GAO

On Strike! How will AI impact the economy, culture, and the future of creativity? – podcast about the 2023 Writers Guild of America strike and perspectives of the use of AI in Hollywood/movies – by the Emerson Collective.

Our Epidemic of Loneliness and Isolation - The US Surgeon General's advisory report on the healing effects of social connection and community (2023).

www.ingramcontent.com/pod-product-compliance
Lightning Source LLC
Chambersburg PA
CBHW050832290526

45792CB00001B/356